The ABC's of Operating Your Salon

CONTENTS

The ABC's of Operating Your Salon

POSITIVE SALON STRATEGIES

ISBN-13: 978-1940128184
ISBN-10: 1940128188

DEDICATION

I dedicate this book to my friends and family for all their encouragement, love and support throughout the years.

ACKNOWLEDGEMENTS

I would like to acknowledge Mimi McCarthy for all her contributions in writing this book, Emmy Intoppa for all the research and efforts put into creating this book, and Richard W. Huntley Jr. for the endless hours put into editing this book to make it a success.

THE ABC'S OF OPERATING YOUR SALON

THE ABC'S OF OPERATING YOUR SALON SECTION ONE

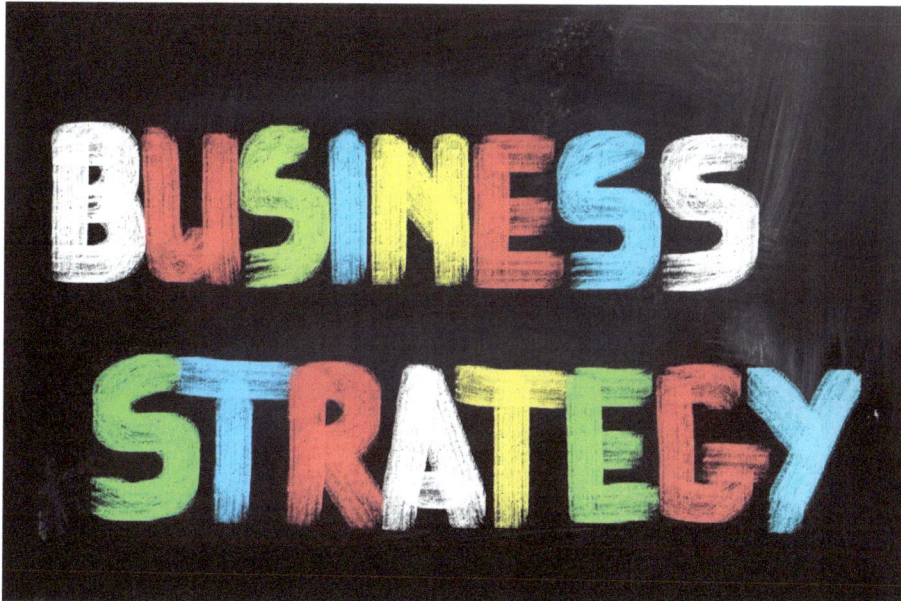

DEVELOPING DISCIPLINE FOR DOLLAR$

In today's economic climate, it is all about outshining your competition, is it not? It is all about establishing a strategy that sets you apart and makes you different. The fact is, salon professionals cannot only excel in the art and science of the beauty profession; they must also excel in the business side of the industry as well.

In this chapter, *The ABC's of Operating Your Salon*, you will learn how to re-motivate yourself as a salon owner.

We will cover how to keep your expenses under control.

You will learn how to create attainable, written goals that are easy to track

We will discuss the importance of having a point of Sale (POS) system in your salon.

We will use this information to create a business action plan.

We will discuss the art of advertising.

We will discuss tips for hiring and retaining loyal staff, and much more.

Once you have completed the first section, you will see that the next sections will continue to build on the information we have already learned.

I have broken it down this way to make large amounts of information more manageable and to help simplify the process. You will want to keep a record of the information we cover as we progress through the trainings so that you have it to look back on and refer to. So let's get started!

In this first section, I want you to start off with identifying the areas in which your salon needs improvement.

Take as much time as you need to answer these questions, because the answers are important in order for you to be able to identify accurately the areas that you may need to change.

First, think back to the time when you were deciding to become a salon owner. Write down as many things as you can remember.

What motivated you in the first place to start a business of your own? For example, was it more free time? Were you looking to be your own boss? Or perhaps it was for investment or retirement purposes. This exercise will help you to re-establish the reasons you went into business in the first place.

_____

_____

_____

_____

What is the ultimate goal for your salon now? The best way to answer this question is by starting with your hoped-for end result because this will help you make a plan of action to build your business to achieve your goals. For example, I want my salon to make me a millionaire so I can have an early retirement.

_____

_____

_____

_____

Jot down some thoughts about what you feel would help you achieve your goals. We will delve into how to set written goals later on in this chapter, but for the moment, what do you think could motivate you to achieve your goals?

_____

_____

_____

_____

Has your experience as an owner been positive, or more trying? Take a few minutes to reflect on this question. It is always helpful to write things down, so make a list of what you have liked, and what you have not liked, about being an owner. For example, I enjoy working with my stylists. I like being my own boss. It has given me more time with my family. I like the freedom it allows me.

My experience as an owner has been···

List the positive things about your salon. For example, I have a fabulous staff. My salon is always presentable and at its best for every client that comes through the door. We pride ourselves on our outstanding customer service, etc.

List the areas where you feel improvement is needed. For example, my retail sales are very weak. I can't seem to get my stylists to up-sell to their clientele. My revenue sales have dropped off since the recession, etc.

_____

_____

_____

_____

We will refer back to all this information later on in this section. First, however, it is time to probe a little deeper.

The next seven questions will help you to identify the strengths and weaknesses in your salon so you can create a plan to accentuate your strengths and to work on your weaknesses. We want to turn your salon's weaknesses into strengths.

1. Do you know what your breakeven is? In other words, do you know how much money your salon needs to generate before you make a profit. Let us say your breakeven amount (the total dollar amount of all your expenses) is $10,000 per month. This is the amount you will need to bring in just to pay your bills. If you know your breakeven amount, enter it here: _____. If you don't know (or are unsure of) your breakeven amount, use the example "Profit and Loss Statement" on page 21 to calculate your breakeven amount and then enter that figure in the space above.

2. Is your payroll in control? Are you paying more than 45% to your stylists? (This percentage would include your total payroll, salary, and/or commissions but exclude payroll taxes). A good rule of thumb to follow is that your payroll should be between 40-45% of your total revenue each week. For example, if your salon's total weekly revenue is $2,000, and you stay between the recommended percentage (the average of which is 43%), your payroll would be $860. Compute that number by multiplying your weekly revenue ($2,000) by 0.43 (43%) for an answer of $860. I have seen too many salons fail due to overpaying staff that the salon cannot afford. Overstaffing will cut into the salon's profit in a big way. Scheduling within your budgetary constraints is very important, especially if you are paying hourly rates and commission fees.

My weekly payroll is:_____.%

Many salons find it difficult to maintain control over their payroll cost, so consider these suggestions:

- Monitor non-technical people on your payroll

- Look at scheduling – are you overstaffing?

- Overtime should be controlled!

- Send people home in slow times

- Offer specials for the slower times of day

- Increase your retail and up-selling sales because these sales will increase your revenue without a big increase in payroll costs

- Remember, the most critical reasons why labor costs are not controlled are due to not training your staff properly, not scheduling your staff properly and not being able to retain team members. These are subjects we will continue to discuss further throughout this book.

I cannot emphasize strongly enough how important these exercises are; it is crucial to know these figures in order to keep your expenses intact. I know many people avoid the task of working through these numbers because it bores them, but it is an essential task for you to complete for your business to be a success.

I have worked with salon owners over the years who did not want to take the time to work through these questions, and time and again, they have told me later they wish they could go back and do it now. So please hang in there with me while we work through these questions.

3. Is your rent too high? If your salon is paying more than 10% of your total monthly revenue on rent, this could present a financial problem. For example, if your total revenue sales are $20,000 per month, then your rent should not exceed $2,000 ($20,000 x 0.10 = $2,000). In this current economy, landlords may be more willing to negotiate rental pricing in order to keep their property leased. I got my landlord to drop my lease $1,000 per month. Hey, it doesn' t hurt to ask. My monthly rent is_____.

4. Is your electric bill too high? I cut my bill in half by purchasing a lock box with a key that only my manager and I had access to. This stopped the rest of the staff from setting the thermostat on a whim.

I also had it programmed to go off at night and back on in the morning. It made such a huge difference in the amount of my electric bill.

5. Do you know where your waste is? Waste is another common problem that can put a salon into serious debt. Over the years, I have witnessed stylists mixing up excess color only to throw half of it down the sink.

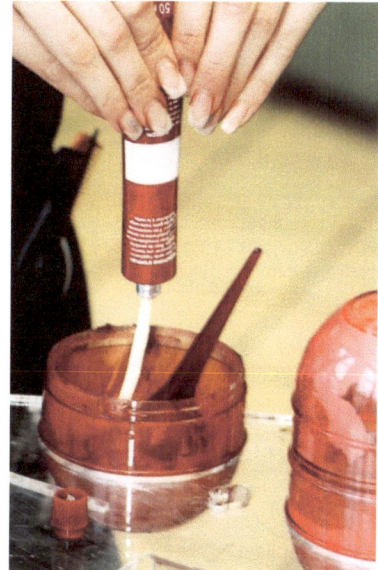

One way to keep on top of this would be to look at how many color services you are doing in a week.

For example, let's say your stylists, on average, use a 2-ounce tube of color for every color service, and your cost for a 2-ounce tube of color is $5. If your salon averages 20 colors a week, then you are averaging 20 tubes of color a week. 20 tubes of color x $5 per tube = $100 of color per week. That should be your cost. If it is much more than that, you have a waste problem.

There are a number of steps you can take to decrease your color waste. Many salons overstock on color. Keep in mind that a salon should only stock 2-3 tubes of all colors and 4-6 tubes of frequently-used colors at one time.

If you haven't done so already:

- You need a system for opened tubes,

- You should educate stylists on how to use color to make colors,

- Don't allow your stylists to waste color or developer by not putting caps back on tightly.

Remember that waste can eventually cause huge profit loss.

6. Is your inventory in control? When ordering supplies, keep in mind you will need to establish a two-week ordering cycle and avoid small orders. Ideally, you should sell the last bottle of shampoo just as the truck delivers the next order.

You don't want to overstock too much inventory because this, too, can cause a loss of profit, so try to order what you are sure you will sell. Remember, sending products back to the warehouse is costly because there is a restocking fee.

Conducting regular inventory is important and will let you know what product is moving and what product is not moving. Regular inventories will also help prevent theft. A good way to track your inventory is by using a Point of Sale system. (We will discuss POS systems in more detail later). You might consider some of these ideas to help you to move excess product:

- Use marketing tools to promote the sale of slower moving items

- Hold a sidewalk sale

- Put together value-added programs

- Make a basket containing your slow-moving products and hold a raffle

To avoid product loss that you cannot account for, train team members to track and control inventory through your computer and take weekly physical counts of all inventory - your staff will take notice.

7. Has your salon ever experienced theft? I have spoken to many salon owners over the years about theft from both staff and clients. In my own salons, I experienced my stylists not checking a client into the computer and taking the money from the client for themselves (this is yet another crucial reason to have a POS system in your salon, which we will cover later).

Voiding out legitimate sales, misuse of coupons, discounts, and gift certificates will all hurt salon profit. When a stylist gives free items or services to friends, relatives, or other team members using the salon's products, this will cut profit. You will find yourself ordering u n n e c e s s a r y i n v e n t o r y .

In my own salon experiences and while working with other salon owners, so many times I have heard the same story: the stylist always has an excuse such as she is not making enough money, or she works harder than anyone else in the salon, and therefore, she feels entitled. I have also heard stylists just blatantly deny it. It always amazes me how much this theft scenario occurs, and stylists often don't think of it as stealing.

If you are experiencing theft, or think you may be, I would highly suggest installing surveillance cameras. The cost for a whole camera system has gone down a great deal over the past few years. This immediately solved my problem with staff theft, and when I posted a sign that cameras were on the premise, it stopped clients as well from taking products. You can view the camera's recordings from your home or when you travel. It is a method to consider implementing to deter stealing and also to provide evidence if a theft does occur.

Now, after you have answered these questions, you need to be able to see what you are paying OUT in expenses versus what your salon is bringing IN. Obviously, this is crucial information to know.

One way to do this is to make a profit and loss list, with all of your expenses listed together and then your revenue, listed as well.

For example, your expenses will include things such as phone, electric, heat, cable, insurance costs, and so on. Your payroll, which is one of your expenses, will fluctuate as your salon grows. But for now, enter your current payroll expense. Your income, on the other hand, will include the money coming in to your salon; for example, revenue from selling your services as well as your products. If you don't already have a method to calculate profit and loss, use the tables on the following pages.

PROFIT AND LOSS STATEMENT

Monthly Expenses

Expenses	JAN	FEB	MAR	APR	MAY	JUNE	JULY	AUG	SEPT	OCT	NOV	DEC
Payroll, Wages, Payroll Taxes, etc												
Debt Loans												
Advertising												
Credit Card Fee												
Product & Sundries												
Bank Charges												
Insurance												
POS Charge												
Miscellaneous												
Licenses												
Office Expenses												
Electric												
Gas												
Phone												
Cable/Internet												
Training & Seminars												
Rent												
Repairs & Maintenance												
Uniform/Clothing												
Other												
TOTAL MONTHLY EXPENSES												

Monthly Sales

Sales	JAN	FEB	MAR	APR	MAY	JUNE	JULY	AUG	SEPT	OCT	NOV	DEC
Service Sales												
Retail Sales												
TOTAL MONTHLY SALES												

Calculate Your Profit/Loss

	JAN	FEB	MAR	APR	MAY	JUNE	JULY	AUG	SEPT	OCT	NOV	DEC
Total Monthly Sales												
- Total Monthly Expenses												
PROFIT/LOSS:												

You should update this profit and loss list on a monthly basis so you can keep close tabs on how much money is coming in and how much is going out. Anything you make above your breakeven amount (which, again, is the total of all your monthly expenses) is *profit!*

Now that you have some actual figures in front of you and you have answered the important questions we discussed, we need to look at how to improve and grow your business internally.

The next step is to complete the following "Salon Evaluation Worksheet" exercise on the next five pages to determine your salon's strengths and weaknesses. This is the place where you can utilize the information about your strengths and weaknesses that your wrote down at the beginning of this s e c t i o n .

SALON EVALUATION WORKSHEET

Directions: Complete the following form to identify and outline the specific Plan of Action for your salon.

Date:

Salon:

Issue Description I: Check the category that best identifies "Needs Improvement."

	Salon Operations
	Increase of Customer Base
	Educational Needs
	Increase of Retail and Service Sales
	Overall Business Development/ In-salon and External Promotions/ Community and Small Business Net-Working

Issue Description II: Circle any boxes that best identify what needs solving.

Salon Operations	Day-to-Day Operations	Increase in Revenue	Customer Service	Staffing	Stylist Retention
Overall Business Development	Outside Promotions	In-Salon Promotions (Staff)	Community Marketing	Cross Promotions	In-Salon Promotions (Client)
Client Needs	New Clients	Repeat Clients	Walk-Outs	Re-do Services	Client Growth
Retail Needs	Sales	Inventory	Product Usage	Back Bar Waste	Team Efforts
Education Needs	Technical Training	Soft Skill Training	New Trends	Product Knowledge	Staff Issues

If Education/Training is required, please define:

Technical Education	Soft Skill Education

Networking Exercise (Check all that are within a 5-mile radius of your salon)

	Wal-Mart, Lowes, Home Depot, or other similar large stores
	Malls
	Nail Salons
	Workout Centers
	Senior Activity Centers
	Retail (Clothing)
	Churches
	Colleges
	High Schools/Junior High Schools
	Restaurants
	Independent Salons and Spas
	Grocery Stores
	Tanning Salons
	Weight Watchers/Curves (or similar)
	Other:

Are you currently running promotions with any of the above?	Yes	No
If "Yes," please list:		

In-Salon Promotion Exercise

List all Current *In-Salon* Promotions	
List all Current *External Salon* Discounts/Coupons	

Do you currently have an e-mail mailing list?	**Yes**	**No**
Do you currently have a Customer Loyalty Program?	**Yes**	**No**
Do you currently have a salon newsletter?	**Yes**	**No**
Are you currently hosti any special events?	**Yes**	**No**

Question	**Always**	**Sometimes**	**Never**
Salon staff provides good customer service.			
Salon staff up-sells services.			
Salon staff up-sells retail.			
Salon experiences walk-out clients.			
Salon experiences re-do services.			
Salon is well-staffed.			
Salon staff has professional appearance.			
Salon holds staff meetings.			
Salon is clean and organized.			

Overall Evaluation

Salon Strengths	Salon Weaknesses
1.	1.
2.	2.
3.	3.
4.	4.
5.	5.

Listed on the next page are various salon topics. Read through the list and check the space that best indicates the priority in which your salon needs support in that area.

Topic	Low Priority	Medium Priority	High Priority
Client Retention			
New Clients			
Increase of Retail Sales			
Internal Staff Problems			
Customer Service Improvement			
Technical Training			
Staff Recruitment			
Salon and Staff Image			
In-Salon Promotions			
Training for Management			
Up-selling Services			
Team Member Mentality			
Community Promotions			
Goal Setting			
Inventory Control			
Marketing/Advertising			
Waste Control			
Other:			

Technical Training Needed:

Additional Education Needed:

List the Top 3 Needs For Your Salon:	1.
	2.
	3.

In Section 3, I provide many great ideas to help you strengthen the weaknesses you' ve just identified in this worksheet. However, before we delve into solutions, it is critical for you **first** to set goals for your salon and staff. The information you have been gathering and writing down in this section will help you to develop a clear understanding of what your salon needs to succeed. With this information in mind, we will learn how to set goals and then how to actually implement a plan to make those goals a reality in your salon. With the bulk of the financial work behind us, I can begin sharing with you so many proven strategies to get you on track!

THE ABC'S OF OPERATING YOUR SALON

SECTION TWO

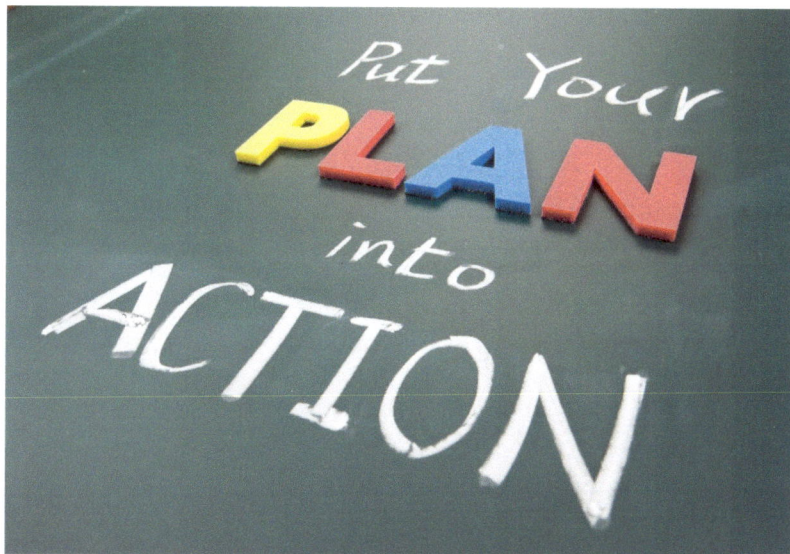

SETTING AND ACHIEVING YOUR GOALS

In this second section of *The ABC's of Operating Your Salon*, we will learn the importance of setting written goals and then we will look at how to execute the proper steps to achieve a positive outcome.

First, let me ask you a question. Are you working in your business or on your business?

If you are working in your business, and you are a licensed cosmetologist, you are probably working behind the chair. This will bring in money, but it will impose limitations on you and your time, which will negatively impact your ability to run a successful business. You must balance your time between working in your salon and working on the business side of your salon.

You need to count on your staff to bring in most of your revenue. It is important that the owner invest most of his or her time running the salon.

It takes time and planning to be successful, and the owner should be developing game plans for the salon. What areas need improving? How am I going to improve them and put a plan in action? This is where the importance of a business plan comes in to play, and it all starts with goals. Setting goals for your salon and staff will allow you to keep track of your business at all times. It will also let you monitor how the salon and staff are performing, taking the guesswork out of evaluations.

Your goals must always be attainable, written, and easy to track.

In order to write your goals, you should identify your salon's uniqueness. Do you offer services that other salons don't offer, or do you offer services that other nearby salons offer as well?

_____

_____

_____

You must know your competition: Do they specialize in chemical services, kids cuts, men's cuts, etc.?

_____

_____

_____

Knowing your competition allows you to determine how you will compete with your competition.

Try to focus on areas other than price. For example, you might offer a 100% money back guarantee.

This always sends the message to the client that you are secure that your services are of the highest quality.

After you have answered the questions above, gather that information together with all the information you just completed in Section One (financial information, "Salon Evaluation Worksheet," etc.). Now that you have determined the areas where you feel your salon can improve and the areas where your salon can succeed – in other words, you have researched your strengths/weaknesses, your finances, and your competition – you should have an idea of possible attainable goals for your salon. Don't forget to write your goals down!

Let's start off with some examples of a goal.

GOAL: I would like to double my hair cutting business within nine months.

You have defined an attainable goal and have given it a time frame.

Next you need to create an action plan that delivers your goal.

An example of the ACTION PLAN could be:

1. With every haircut, clients will receive a free sample-sized product of their choice.

2. We will create a loyalty stamp card for each client that states, after five haircuts, the sixth haircut is free.

Let me share another example of a creative action plan. A salon I worked with found their niche by advertising that they specialized in the expertise of cutting long hair. How many times have we heard the horror stories and complaints that a client asked the stylist to cut an inch and she took off three inches instead? As a result, many people with long hair won't get their hair cut on a regular basis. This salon made a killing in accentuating a service that many other salons were weak in.

They tracked their business with a POS system, which is something I discuss in the next segment, and they tripled their business in six-month's time.

Another example of a GOAL may be: I want to increase my color business by 20 percent in the next six months.

Again, you have defined a specific goal and have given it a measurable time frame.

Now you need to write down an ACTION PLAN on how you plan to achieve this goal.

It may look like this.

1. Offer advanced color education for the staff.

2. Offer luncheon specials for the working woman. In this lunchtime special package, the client will get five-seven foils with her haircut and will receive a free, deep protein conditioner. You can offer snacks to make it even more inviting.

3. Put together events or incentives for your staff to up-sell a color service to clients who are scheduled for just a haircut.

4. Give a free bottle of shampoo when clients get a color service done.

5. Plan a color extravaganza day – this is a great way to build new color clients. You may want to offer 25-50% off your color services for new clients. Make sure you rebook them for their next appointment by offering them $5.00 off their next visit when they book that day.

This may sound expensive, but remember that a happy and content color client will become a loyal client, and loyal clients grow your bottom line. There are so many ideas you can come up with when you are writing your action plan to meet your goals that will separate you from your competition.

For example:

   ▪ Offer 5-minute massages and deep conditioning with every shampoo.

- Offer a wine and cheese after-hours for the working woman and man.

- Advertise a lunch special for the working woman: Get your nails and hair done while having lunch provided by the salon.

- Offer a pampering, moisturizing paraffin hand treatment while you get your hair done.

- Give out brochures listing all of your services to existing clients so that they can pass them out to friends.

- Have a "Children's Day" haircut program.

- Offer a "Try Me" special on your least- requested service, such as a complimentary deep protein treatment with every haircut.

- Offer a limited time "Bring a Friend" discount.

- Hold a "Mousse and Gel Clinic" in your salon to demonstrate spiking and scrunching methods.

- Think of a creative promotion for each and every holiday. Sound impossible? It's not.

- Offer a senior citizen's special.

- Pass out brochures at your local shopping mall.

- Start a salon newsletter.

In the next section, Section 3, you will find many more ideas that you can use when you are developing your action plans. Truly, the ideas are endless. Once you find your niche and your uniqueness, elaborate on it as much as possible!

When you are ready to start writing goals and action plans for your salon, I have included an easy-to-use "Salon Plan of Action" table on the next several pages for your convenience.

Salon Plan of Action

Write Your Goals and Action Plans

In-Salon Promotions *(Events/Extravaganzas)*
Goal:
Action Plan:

In-Salon Promotions *(Retail Promotions)*
Goal:
Action Plan:

Outside-Salon Promotions - Coupons/Discounts

Goal:

Action Plan:

In-Salon Promotions *(In-Salon Service Specials)*

Goal:

Action Plan:

	Outside-Salon Promotions - Community Marketing *(Promotions Within the Community)*
	Goal:
	Action Plan:

So we have talked about setting goals for your salon; now we need to look at goal setting with your stylists. In order to accurately set goals, you will need to communicate regularly with every stylist so that you can evaluate their overall performance.

For example, some questions you will want to ask are:

- What are the stylist's strengths?

- Where are the areas that need improvement?

- Does the stylist sell retail?

- Does the stylist up-sell services?

- Could the stylist improve his or her speed?

Have you set goals for your staff? Are you having weekly, one-on-one meetings with each of your staff members to set (and review) goals that will enable them to increase their pay checks, and thereby in return, increase the salon's overall revenue?

I am a firm believer in setting up goals and incentives for your stylists so that they have a plan going forward.

You may want to start the meeting with your stylist by having her make a dream list of the things she wants to buy in the future when she begins making more money.

Another positive approach to take with your stylist is to break down the dollar goals into something such as "all you have to do is sell x number of products a day to reach your weekly dollar goal," and so on.

Each week, you will need to go over what direction you and your stylist's pre-established goals are headed and then take whatever action you need to turn it in the right direction. Before each one-on-one weekly meeting, make sure you have one to two items planned out that you want to focus on with each stylist. Make sure you have reviewed each stylist's numbers prior to the meeting.

Make sure your goals for your salon coincide with your stylist's goals. Always have a plan that will involve praising and recognizing each stylist to keep the meeting positive. During the meeting, for example, let's say you had set a previous goal with your stylist that she would introduce three new clients to a color service, but at the end of the week she had accomplished only one. You should first ask yourself was the stylist part of setting this goal or was it the owner or manager who set this goal?

Always let the stylist tell you what she thinks she can attain. It is very important that the stylist be accountable for her own goals. It also increases the chance that the goal will be met, since it was not forced on the stylist, and she believes the goal could be attainable. Once she has set her goals with the owner or manager, the one-on-one meetings will involve the owner or manager coaching the stylist on how to meet her goals. For example, create promotions such as 10% off color services for all new clients. This will allow the stylist to have a tool with which to start the conversation about up-selling services with the client. This type of goal setting and follow-up teaches the stylist how to be in control of giving herself a pay raise.

Use a worksheet when you have your stylist one-on-one meetings; it ensures you clarify and document what your stylist has been achieving and the new goals that are being set. I have included an example of a "One-on-One Meeting Worksheet" that you may want to use.

ONE -ON- ONE MEETING WORKSHEET

Name of Stylist:

Manager/Owner:

Date:

SERVICES	PRICE	TOTAL # DONE	TOTAL $ MADE	NEW GOAL #	FORECASTED $ INCREASE	SALON GOAL
Women's Haircut and Finish						
Color Services						
Highlight Services						
Highlight - Lowlight						
Glossing						
5-7 Foils						
Blow Dries						
Kid's Cuts						
Men's Cuts						
Texturizing (Perming)						
Straightening						
Accessorizing The Hair						
Deep Protein Treatments						
Deep Moisturizing Treatments						
Waxing						
Facials						
Teeth Whitening						

During your meeting with your stylist, you may also find it helpful to use this next piece titled "Who Are You?" to help your stylist identify which type of person she would rather be. My stylists always found it very informative to see the bottom line $ figures in black and white!

WHO ARE YOU?

Negative Nellie works a total of 30 hours per week and serves five clients a day, five days a week. She is always bored and gives her clients minimal customer service. She never has goals or a plan of action to grow her business. She gossips and creates drama in the salon. People don' t like being around her negativity. She never hands out her business cards when out in the community. It is just a job for Nellie, not a career. She hardly ever gets requests, even though she has been there over six months.

5 clients a day at $20 per haircut = $100 per day service sales

$100 per day x 5 days per week = $500 gross service sales per week

If the salon is paying Nellie 45% commission on her gross service sales, then:

45% x $500 = $225 (this is Nellie' s gross weekly pay from service sales)

She never sells products, so she earns $0 in product commission sales

$225 (gross service sales pay) + $0 (product commission sales) = **$225 gross pay per week**

Fabulous Fran also works 30 hours per week and also serves fi e clients a day, fi e days a week. She arrives at work dressed well, with make-up on and hair fashionably arranged. Fran values her job and calls it a career. She always treats her clients with care.

Fran believes one can never pamper enough. She wants her clients to always look and feel their best. Fran always has new ideas, hairstyles, color, highlights and cuts for her clients. She takes pride in her work and always goes the extra mile to ensure her client has a fabulous experience. She talks to her clients about products that would help their hair to perform at its best. She always offers a *solution,* not a *product,* for hair needs (I explain this concept in my book *Retailing in Action*). Fran is always positive and a team player.

Fran up-sells each $20 hair cut into an additional $70 color service (haircut + up-sell = $90) so:

5 clients a day x $90 service = $450 per day service sales

$450 per day x 5 days per week = $2,250 gross service sales per week

If the salon is paying Fran 45% commission on her gross service sales, then:

45% x $2,250 = $1,012.50 (this is Fran's gross weekly pay from service sales)

Fran sets a goal of selling five, $15 products per day. $15 x 5 per day = $75 per day. $75 per day x 5 days per week = $375 product sales per week

If the salon is paying Fran 10% commission on her product sales, then:

10% x $375 = $37.50 (this is Fran's weekly product commission pay)

$1,012.50 (gross service sales pay) + $37.50 (product commission sales) = **$1,050 gross pay per week**

And by all means, don't forget to make your salon a fun atmosphere for your staff! They are more likely to do well and be loyal to you if they enjoy their working environment.

For example, have theme days in your salon where everyone dresses up as their favorite celebrity. It adds a fun environment, and the stylists will love it. Let them be a part of the voting process as to what themes they would like. This encourages staff participation and support as well.

When you and your staff enjoy being at your salon, your clients will enjoy it too. One of the things I did to create a fun atmosphere was to get a popcorn machine - one of the old fashioned ones for $200.00 - and I offered popcorn on Saturdays and a free picture of children after their haircut.

As I have said before, the ideas are endless. In upcoming chapters, I discuss creating the "aha moment," and I offer many more exciting ideas to keep clients interested and always wondering what you will be doing next.

It is so important for the owner to know how to manage his or her time wisely in order to ensure the best outcome. If you are fi   time management to be a problem for you, create a goal and action plan to improve it! Make sure your staff is properly trained and offering the best customer service possible. I sometimes hired a mystery shopper to come into my salon and document everything she witnessed (many companies out there offer this service). I then sat down with my staff, both individually and as a group, to go over the positive statements and how we were to improve on the weak areas.

I am a firm believer that everything we set out to do starts with a dream; we turn the dream into goals, and then build a business plan based on our goals. Remember, **goals must always be written, attainable, and easy to track.** Taking control back is one of the most empowering actions you can do for your business. I have always said the antidote to fear is knowledge. This book is designed to do just that: give you back control and put you back in charge.

Remember you have to know where you are at currently and then where you want to go. Written goals will help you stay focused. Do not overwhelm yourself. Have fun!

In the next section, we will be learning the art of advertising on a shoestring budget. I will show you creative ways to get new clients in your door without spending a lot. I will give you lists of ideas, some old and some new, for creating new promotions. I will also offer ideas on how to keep your current clients from going to your competition. My hope is that all this information will get your own creative juices flowing as well, as you create new plans to grow your business.

THE ABC'S OF OPERATING YOUR SALON

SECTION THREE

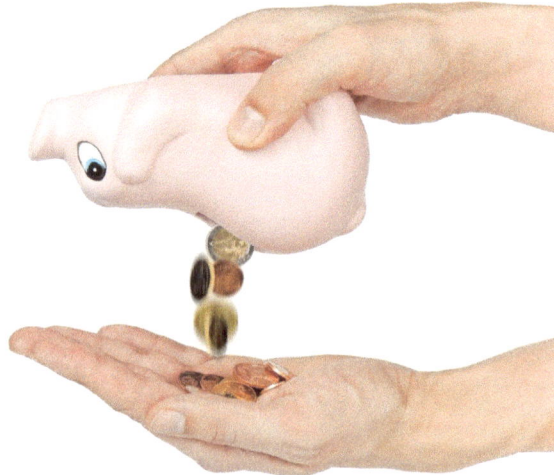

ADVERTISING ON A SHOESTRING BUDGET

In this section, we will be discussing the art of advertising on a shoestring budget. Advertising: a subject that causes many people to sigh! It seems overwhelming, but it doesn' thave to be.

We will learn why a Point of Sale system is so important for your salon.

We will discuss some incentive programs that can help your business grow.

We want to ensure that you are using your money wisely to create the most revenue and, thereby, increase the value of your salon.

I can't tell you how many salons owners and managers I have talked to who don't have any idea what advertising plan is working best and what is bringing back customers. They don't know where they are wasting money.

Let's work to bring the advertising of your salon from an expense to an investment.

You need to measure and track the success of each component of the advertising that you do. This is where a POS (or point of sale) system can be very helpful. It allows you to track all the promotions and/or coupons you have sent out and then tracks them when they come back in. You are able to track which ones bring in new customers and you can even see which are bringing lost clients back in again. This knowledge allows you to focus your time on what works and not waste your time (and money) on what does not.

There are many companies that offer POS systems. You can find these companies on the internet. However, I highly recommend that you research POS systems that are geared for salon use.

There are also marketing companies that you can hire to go into your POS system and do mailings at a very affordable price to areas in the select zip codes of your choice. At your request, such marketing companies can also go into your POS system and send gift certificates to all your women who get haircuts only, offering money off when they try a color service with you.

Through your POS system, these marketing companies can also find clients that have not been back for three, six, or nine months and send them a "we miss you letter" with a $5.00 off certificate to entice them back in. They also offer e-mail clubs where they can do extensive e-mail blasts to potential clients and to new clients. The list is endless with companies like this once you have a POS system.

The POS system will give you an end-of-the-day report every evening after you close your salon with all the services your staff did that day separated out into different categories.

A POS system keeps track of what your retention rate is (in other words, how many of your customers keep coming back); it keeps track for your salon as a whole, and it will also keep track of each stylist's record of retention as well. This will allow you to see which of your stylists are bringing back clients and which ones are not. You can then meet with that stylist and reevaluate why she is not bringing back the clients she has previously done.

The POS system will keep records of any redo's that may have happened during the month. It also gives you weekly and monthly reports to view at your convenience.

If you don't already have some form of POS system, I highly recommend you investigate a system that would suit your needs.

Okay, so now that we've covered the importance of being able to track the effectiveness of your advertising, let's look at cost-effective ways to advertise.

Do you find your salon is successful in bringing in new customers? Are you able to bring in clients at a regular rate? Do you have a sufficient number of customers, or are you struggling to get them in the door? And, of course, once you do get customers in the door, are you able to keep them coming back?

Take a moment to jot down your answers to these questions.

Building a successful client base does not have to be complicated. It takes a lot of hard work and preparation, but when it comes to getting new clients, you don't have to spend all of your resources in hopes of getting the return you want.

One of the most cost-effective ways to build your clientele is to rely on your best customers to bring in more customers. This requires that you develop a plan and make sure you continue to see it to fruition. Let's just think for a moment.

What new customer do you think is more valuable, one who finds your business by chance or one who finds your business because a friend told her about it?

In general, referred customers are more valuable because they already have a level of trust with your stylists and salon, and, also importantly, it cost little or nothing to get them in the door. Therefore, from the minute that customer walks through the door, each sale you make to her is more profitable for you.

So how do you develop a referral system that works for your business?

Start by providing the best possible service for your existing customers, especially those customers that come in on a regular basis. How to provide the best customer service is a topic we go into in more depth further on in this book.

Next, review your incentive programs. Do you have a good incentive program set up for your top customers? For example, when these customers tell their friends and family about you, they should receive something from you such as a discounted product or service. If your clients love your business, they MAY tell other people about you, but if they love YOU, and you make it worth their while, they WILL tell other people about you.

One popular incentive program that I have seen many salons use with great success is the referral business card program. The cards are intended for stylists to hand out to each client after their service. That card should have a space for your client to fill in her name and address. The referral card offers the potential new client an incentive to come in, such as 50% off your first visit. Make the offer as intriguing and as enticing as possible.

Each time a new client brings in the card with your current client's name, you will mail your current client something as a thank you. I used to mail them a $5.00 gift certificate to be used at their next service. Everyone wins with this promotion: the new client, the current client, and the salon. This starts to build a strong client base with very little expense to you.

Every time a client goes out of their way to send us a friend or family member it is a tremendous opportunity for us to grow our business, not to mention the positive message our loyal client is giving by sending us a referral. But what is one loyal customer sending us referrals on a regular basis really worth? Use the following equation to see.

Follow steps 1-5, plugging in your own numbers.
(See the example below.)

1. Value of each guest (your current average ticket)

2. Guest refers three people (current average ticket x 3)

3. Each guest visits eight times a year (line 2 x 8)

4. Number of years as guest (average is 5 years) (line 3 x 5-year average)

5. What are they worth?

For Example:

1. Value of each client (your current average ticket) = **$40.00**

2. Your client refers three people: **3 X $40.00 = $120.00**

3. Each client visits eight times a year: **$120.00 X 8 = $960.00**

4. Number of years as a client (average is 5 years): **$960.00 X 5 = $4,800.00 That is the worth of a referral.**

As you can see, you should never underestimate the value of referrals! So, keeping in mind that your cost for bringing in referred clients is little to nothing, you can see why one of the best forms of advertising is word of mouth. Let your clients do the work and you focus on the best customer service possible. Again, in the next chapters, I show you how to give the client the best possible experience ever, making her want to tell the world about your salon.

Remember, statistics show that 80% of the reason a client returns to your salon is because of the experience they had while being serviced at your salon. The other 20%

of customers say they return because of the actual service done. A client who is happy with your salon and services is more likely to forgive an occasional haircut that it not of the same quality that they are accustomed to (because we all have our bad days), but they will look elsewhere if they have received poor customer service.

Another great way of advertising with little or no expense is to involve your salon in the community.

Become a sponsor for your local youth sports teams, for example, the little league team.

Hold cut-a-thons for your favorite charity. A lot of newspapers and radio stations will advertise for free when it is done for charities. For example, when I owned my salon, I would support breast cancer awareness week. I would write a letter to the breast cancer association and let them know that I was supporting their charity for a specific week or month with a portion of the salon' s proceeds going to the charity. In return, they would send me a letter to verify the event. I would submit the letter to all local advertising venues, and my salon would receive advertising from radio stations on the hour or in print in the local paper.

Don' t overlook networking with other companies in your area. For example, network with Weight Watchers and/or Curves, offering their clients 10% off their first visit - or every visit; it can be whatever you choose.

Try linking up with a local boutique to do hair and makeup for their next fashion show.

Offer military and other service people a VIP business card to keep in their wallet to use when getting their haircut, offering them a discount, such as 15% off their haircuts.

Make up special packages for nurses and medical staff at the hospitals near you. I was very successful in doing this in my salons.

Make out VIP cards for students, then hand them out to all your teenage clients to give to their friends.

You can also visit schools and offer a free demonstration on extensions, hairstyling, etc. This can be particularly lucrative before prom time.

The following handout, "Marketing Business Tools," offers more detail on some of the advertising and marketing suggestions I just discussed, and there are more suggestions as well that you may find useful.

MARKETING BUSINESS TOOLS

VIP CARD

- Customize the card with your particular salon information as well as the specific discount that you want to provide.

- Use these cards as local business discount cards within a nearby shopping center.

- VIP cards can also be used for military, police, firemen, and nurses.

SENIOR DISCOUNT FLYER

- Distribute or post a flyer in your salon to promote senior business hours.

- Use the days or hours in your salon that are slowest to promote this event. (Mornings and early afternoons usually work best – but avoid weekends, as these are your busiest days). The idea is to build business at a time when you normally have a lull in services.

- If you are interested in distributing this flyer, check with local senior community centers or churches.

COLOR EXTRAVAGANZA FLYER

- Pass them out locally.

- Provide one to all clients who visit your salon.

- The idea is to plan an event that promotes color services to your clients who normally do not have them done.

- Make it a fun event with your staff.

- Promote an event like this weeks in advance to build momentum and interest.

SALON NEWSLETTER

- Great tool for promoting services and retail to your existing clients.

- Create a monthly or bi-monthly newsletter to inform clients of retail promotions, service specials and salon events.

- Feature a specific product each issue or even talk about your staff.

- Take the opportunity to promote all you offer in your salon.

- You can create them and print them, or you can distribute them electronically, which will cost you nothing.

OTHER MARKETING OPPORTUNITIES

- Check with the Parent-Teacher groups at your local schools.

  - Student organizations (student governments, pep teams, orchestra and band) are always looking to build funds and retain sponsors for events.

  - Schools have athletic departments that offer great promotion opportunities – sponsor/host the sports teams and cheerleading league.

  - Student papers are always looking for businesses to post ads in their publications. (At prom time, place an ad about up-dos. For spring, feature a coupon for highlighting services. Offer an honor roll discount, rewarding students with great grades. Get creative, because the possibilities are endless. Don't underestimate the power of using a school paper— they offer you great exposure to teens).

- The same goes for college newspapers and university publications.

  - Once again, you have a direct link to a target audience.

▢ Offer a discount when students present their college ID card in your salon.

▢ If the college has a radio station, you can purchase on-air promotions or ads for a great price.

▢ See if there is a dormitory council. Each semester, new students move into the dorms – usually these students are given information packets that include coupons for local businesses in the direct vicinity of the college.

• Contact owners and managers of apartments and rentals. Ask to put your salon's information in the welcome packet new renters receive upon moving in.

• Community publications are great for your business for two reasons.

▢ The smaller the publication, the more inexpensive it is to place an ad.

▢ They focus on targeting an audience in a concentrated area. In a small community paper, you'll have more of a chance of being noticed.

• Cross-promote with local businesses in your area.

▢ Tanning salons

▢ Nail salons

▢ Bridal boutiques

▢ Fitness centers, etc.

▢ Many of these businesses are looking to cross-promote with you as well.

▢ Knock on some doors and see what opportunities are available to you. Just keep in mind that the business next door is not always your competition – chances are you share some of the same potential clients.

- Churches host a variety of events throughout the year.

  - Check to see if they publish their events in a paper or newsletter to their members. You may be surprised how many parishes in your neighborhood are willing to take advantage of any assistance or promotions you can offer.

There are so many cost-effective ways to market your business. The ideas are endless! Be creative and make it fun.

Another hidden secret I want to be sure you are aware of is a wonderful incentive program, which because I found it to be so successful in my salons, I offer it directly on my website. This program utilizes vacation certificates as an incentive to encourage clients to spend more in your salon. I also used them as performance incentives for my staff.

Vacation certificates are not associated in any way with time-share properties. The certificates work so well because the cost is minimal for you to purchase, yet they have a high-perceived value to your customers and staff. The way it works is the salon owner buys the certificates for only $4-5 per certificate, depending on the volume purchased. Each certificate is for a three day, two night hotel stay and is valued up to $180, depending on the geographical location and hotel selection.

You can utilize these certificates to provide your customers, and staff, with a meaningful reward that they can actually use.

You will find that when you give out these vacation certificates:

- You will increase your sales by motivating your team to out-perform.

- You will retain your top performers.

- You will create repeat business: existing clients will have an incentive to return more frequently and to spend more money each time.

- You will attract new clients and generate referrals.

- You will outperform your competition and create a unique position in the marketplace.

- Give your customers more than they expect by increasing the value of the service you provide to them, and they will love you and your business for it.

On my website, www.PositiveSalonStrategies.com, click on "Vacation Certificates" for more information and great ideas on how to use the incentive certificates.

Remember, knowing what advertising plans, referral plans, and incentive programs are working best for you is very important. You do not want to waste your resources on programs that are not providing a good return for your salon. Your time and money are valuable, and you want to make them count for all they are worth!

On the next pages you will find three "handouts" I have used over the years to give you even more promotional ideas; take from them any suggestions that sound good to you, and of course, add your own ideas too!

The Fabulous Forty

Stumped for fresh ideas when it comes to creating new promotions? Here's a starter set of 40 ideas. Some are old, some are new, some may appeal to you and some may not. Use this material as food for thought to get your own creative juices flowing.

1. Hold a cut-a-thon for charity.

2. Link up with a local boutique to do hair and makeup for their next fashion show.

3. Sponsor a Little League or Walk-A-Thon team.

4. Suggest a free home care assembly program at local high schools.

5. Make news and send out press releases covering it.

6. Hold a seasonal hair fashion show with refreshments.

7. Write a letter to the editor and sign it with your own name and the name of your salon.

8. Donate a hair styling or perm for a local charity auction.

9. Put your salon's menu up on college and church bulletin boards.

10. Buy several small display ads in the newspaper instead of one larger ad.

11. Advertise in the classifieds.

12. Do a bulk mailing introducing your salon and its services to non-clients in your area.

13. Offer one of your local female newscasters - or all of them - a cosmetic make-over, and then get a photographer to take pictures and mail out the press release.

14. Suggest yourself as a radio talk show guest to discuss the latest salon techniques.

15. Hold a series of weekly in-salon seminars on makeup and hair care.

16. Request information about co-op advertising from manufacturers whose products you retail.

17. Hold a senior citizen's special.

18. Order salon t-shirts and offer them at a discounted price to your clients or use them as crossover marketing.

19. Pass out brochures at your local shopping mall.

20. Advertise in the yellow pages.

21. Run a sweepstakes, perhaps with a salon gift certificate as a prize.

22. Offer a "TRY ME" special on your least requested secondary service.

23. Give a limited time "BRING A FRIEND" discount.

24. Offer reasonably priced catered lunches or sandwiches over the noon hour for the working woman.

25. Have a "CHILDREN'S DAY" haircut program.

26. Give brochures listing all your services to existing clients.

27. Cross-market retail items. Use a pretty ribbon to tie a vented brush around a bottle of shampoo.

28. Hold a mousse and gel "clinic" to demonstrate spiking and scrunching methods.

29. Invite your newspaper's lifestyles editor to lunch and a tour of the salon.

30. Start a salon newsletter.

31. Network with professionals in other businesses through your chamber of commerce.

32. Check with other local small businesses about swapping mailing lists.

33. Start sending birthday cards to clients.

34. Spotlight a different retail item every week.

35. Think of a creative promotion for every holiday. Sound impossible? It's not.

36. Start changing your displays and smaller items of décor on a regular basis.

37. Promote your most positive points by offering a gift if you fail to live up to them. We pride ourselves on our scheduling···we promise you $5 off every 15 minutes of waiting time."

38. Motivate your staff with a reward for increased business.

39. Hold an anniversary party. Send out press releases to community news editors.

40. Read the "business ledger" section of the newspaper and send $10 gift certificates with letters of congratulations to people whose promotions are announced.

Seventeen Ways to Win the Working Woman

Have you "stretched" enough to reach the working woman? Or have you thought of her as "just another salon client" and made no attempt to offer her something your competition hasn't considered? Here are seventeen promotional ideas for winning over the working woman. We hope you've tried some of them already. Why not make a point of checking off the ones that might be right for your salon? Then prioritize the ideas you've checked and make plans to put them into action. Always remember that success is something that you make happen!

1. **Offer lunch or snacks** - this doesn't have to be a complicated operation. If you're near a coffee shop, perhaps you can make arrangements for delivery. Or you could give clients the option of a pre-ordered box lunch and pack the lunches yourself. Many women can't afford the time to visit the salon and fit in lunch too.

2. **Offer a simultaneous service package** - promote a "working woman's special," promising to deliver a cut, blow dry and manicure all in just an hour appointment. Then coordinate the manicurist's schedule so she'll be working on the client's nails during the styling.

3. **Set up wireless internet for your business clients** - so they can work while they wait for their appointment or while they are getting a time-consuming service.

4. **Suggest a demonstration for your local woman's business group** - a talk on "dressing for success" or "office grooming" will usually be welcome.

5. **Consider changing your hours** – many salons are reaching the working woman by opening earlier, closing later and/or adding Sunday hours.

6. **Network with a clothing store for a shopper's special** – this is a good promotion for Thursday evenings when shops have late hours. You could offer clients a 15% discount, good for only that same night, at a local shop, asking the shop to do the same for you.

7. **Set special business women's hours during which there will be an image consultant at no charge** – not only will you be offering working women a benefit, the image consultant can sell perms and color for you.

8. Link up with a secretarial service or free-lance secretary – you can offer this service – if booked in advance – for women who want to catch up on correspondence or other work while they are in the salon.

9. **Promote pedicures** – a discounted pedicure is hard for women to resist – especially for those whose jobs call for a lot of time spent standing.

10. **Fill your reception area with a lot of mail order catalogues** – then get the word out that clients can shop by mail in the salon. You could even photocopy extra order forms for their convenience. If you have free internet service (as was mentioned earlier), your clients can order from their laptops or mobile devices.

11. **Develop a tie-in with a local spa or health club** – today's working woman is often health and figure conscious.

12. **Give an "on-time" guarantee** – women with jobs are on tight schedules. Promise a big percentage off the total service bill if a client's waiting time is more than so many minutes. This is a good gimmick, as it proclaims your faith in the smooth running of your salon.

13. **Hold a stress seminar** – you may want to barter with an expert to demonstrate stress-relief techniques in the salon.

14. **Do a mailing to large companies for Secretary's Day** – write directly to the company's president, offering specials for Secretary's Day gifts. You might offer

$20 gift certificates with increasing discounts (i.e., boss pays $18 each for 3-5, $15 each for 5-10, $14 each for more than 10).

15. **Arrange for babysitting service** - setting an area aside for tots (and having a sitter present) will attract working mothers.

16. **Hold a drawing for a computer or microwave** - both of these items are coveted by most businesswomen.

17. **Offer a wine and cheese after hours special** - what a nice way to end the day, especially when her special service is accompanied by a relaxing scalp and neck massage.

Male Call

Promotional ideas to bring men into your salon

1. **Team Power** - get the press involved with free "hair makeovers" for top players on any sports teams that have high visibility.

2. **Celebrity Clout** - barter salon services with local anchormen or disc jockeys in return for endorsements.

3. **Father and Son Day** - give dads a half-price haircut if they bring in their son for a haircut at the same time.

4. **Boss's Day** - print up special gift certificates for bosses and sell them for a gift.

5. **Members Only** - set aside a day when specific club members (Elks, Rotary, etc.) receive discounts.

6. **For Men Only** - schedule a men's seminar with advice and information on men's services and hairpieces.

7. **King for a Day** - offer "the works" (cut, beard or mustache trim, facial, manicure) at a special package price.

8. **Men's Night** - set aside time one evening a week that is for men only.

9. **Gift for the Groom** - give "the works" free to the groom who brings in all of his ushers and best man.

10. **Two for One** - two for one special for any man who comes in with a (male) pal.

THE ABC'S OF OPERATING YOUR SALON

SECTION FOUR

HIRING AND RETAINING LOYAL STAFF

One of the most frequently asked questions I get from salon owners is: "How do I get my staff to work hard, be loyal to my salon, and not leave, taking their clientele with them?" Most salon owners put a great deal of time and money into training staff. What I hear all too often is that the work ethic of some people in these current, younger generations is not acceptable. I hear frequent complaints that this generation has a lack of understanding that it takes hard work to build a client base because there is a certain "sense of entitlement" that things will be handed to them on a silver platter. In addition, there is an expectation that a lot of money will be made quickly. When I owned my salons, it always baffled me that my staff thought I was a millionaire and should offer them the moon. Wow! As salon owners, we know so differently.

In my own salons, I decided to put a plan into action that helped me out immensely. It did not, 100 percent, take away this problem of turnover and lack of loyalty, but it reduced it by at least 70 percent.

The plan starts right from the interviewing process. As the owner, you need to have an organized plan of action when choosing the right candidate for your salon. Here are some points to take into consideration.

First and foremost, create an employee handbook with all the rules of the salon, your expectations, and a consequence list for prospective staff to read and understand and then sign when they are hired. Your handbook should explain in detail a list of unacceptable actions that are against salon policy and the expectant consequences of those particular actions. The consequence may be one verbal warning, a written warning, or grounds for immediate termination. You need to be clear about what the exact repercussion will be; for example, if a staff member receives three verbal warnings, a written warning follows with a probation period. If the action continues, termination will follow. If you believe that certain unacceptable behaviors should result in immediate termination with no prior warning (such as theft), that needs to be clearly stated. Keep a very detailed file on each employee in case you will ever need it down the road for verifying information, for unemployment, lawsuits, etc. Having a clear list of unacceptable behaviors and subsequent consequences leaves nothing to be misunderstood if the inappropriate behavior occurs.

I found that having such a handbook helped my staff to feel I was being fair with each of them, and not "playing favorites." This was especially helpful in the more gray areas of my expectations. For example in my salons I would not tolerate gossip or back stabbing, and there was no room for prima donnas. I would give a warning for this behavior, and my staff quickly realized that no one was exempt from this expectation.

In addition to an employee handbook ensuring that my staff and I had a clear under-standing of the salon policies, it also provided written material for me to refer back to with my staff, showing them that they signed it, indicating they understood the policies and had agreed to follow them. It also minimized staff members trying to use the excuse that they did not know that a certain policy or expectation existed.

The following information is a handout I would give to members of my salon management team to provide them with guidelines of what my expectations were. I believed it was very important for a staff to understand the reasons for having an employee handbook and to ensure that we were all on the same page.

THE IMPORTANCE OF AN EMPLOYEE HANDBOOK

- If your team does not know the "rules," then they cannot be held responsible when they don' t measure up to your expectations.

- Team member handbooks must include all the salon' s policies and procedures.

- Each team member should receive a copy of the handbook and sign a receipt stating that they have read and understand the content of the handbook.

- If employees know the rules and vision of the salon, then they will feel confident to make decisions.

- An employee handbook is a communication tool designed to empower employers, managers and employees with a consistent approach to accomplishing their daily tasks.

- It provides a set of policies, procedures, forms and work routines that convey the pulse of the organization.

- A properly developed manual focuses everyday business communications between employees and managers on what is really important to get the job done.

- This handbook is the first step in the implementation process of communicating the policies and procedures within a salon.

- Use an employee manual as a starting point.

- Create an easy to read policy guide with descriptions as a reference for employees.

- Hold staff meetings to give guidance, direction and training for policies or procedures.

- Create huddles so all employees have a voice in the implementation process.

- Have coaching sessions for employees who require more involvement in the implementation process.

- Create a reward system to assist in the support of the implementation process.

- A key aspect of a reward system is to recognize compliance efforts so that employees perceive that it is in their best interest to support policies and procedures.

- Rewards do not need to be costly or time consuming.

- Involve team members so they "buy in."

- Award suggestions:

    Best Attendance Award

    Best Dressed Award

    Employee of the Month Award

 Ø Best Customer Service Award

 Ø Early Bird Award

    Best Team Player

    Best Award for Up-selling

    Best Award for Retailing

───────────────────────────────

Because I believe so strongly in putting things in writing, I used a "discipline sheet" as a guide in my salons. I am including it here so that you may use it as a reference when you are creating your own written policies and procedures. I used to put the form on the wall in the lunch room so everyone could view it whenever they wanted to. I could then answer any questions my stylists might have.

DISCIPLINE SHEET

The Written Warning

- A written warning serves as a formal notice that a serious infraction has occurred.

- Written warnings should state the nature of the offense, method of correction, and action to be taken if offense is repeated.

- A written warning also serves to gain the employee's agreement that this will be the last time that a problem needs to be addressed.

The Verbal Warning

- Example:

"As you were informed prior to your employment here, this salon has a career apparel of black and white clothing, which you are not dressed in. I will provide you with a black smock to wear today during your shift, however, starting tomorrow I'll expect that you will be in proper salon attire."

The Final Warning

- Its purpose is to inform the employee that his/her job is in jeopardy of being lost.

- Example of a final warning:

"You were scheduled to work this Saturday. When you did not appear at the salon, the manager called you to find out if you had planned on reporting to work that day. You stated that you would be in within the hour. You failed to show or call the salon. If this situation repeats

itself, it will be considered job abandonment and you will be terminated from this salon."

Reasons for Warnings

- The employee does not meet performance criteria

- The employee has violated your policies and procedures

- The employee is in constant conflict with you or others they work with

- The employee consistently has personal problems that are interfering with his/her job performance

Before Giving a Warning, Ask Yourself These Questions

- Does the employee understand his/her job responsibilities?

- Does the employee understand the consequences of negative behavior?

- Did the employee understand and sign the salon policy handbook?

During the Warning Process

- Make sure you have proof of poor performance

- Does the employee's explanation have merit?

- Have you done everything to give the employee the benefit of the doubt?

Types of Discipline

- Consequence chart

- Coaching sessions

- Counseling sessions

- Verbal reminders

- Increase "check-ups" on job performance

- Oral reprimand (verbal warning)

- Written reprimand (written warning)

- Temporarily sending them home

- Reducing hours

- Temporary probation

- Termination

For example, after 3 verbal warnings and 2 written warnings, then the last step before termination is suspension

- The purpose of the suspension is to let the team member know the seriousness of the problem

- The suspension should be used as a "cooling off " period in which to resolve the problem if possible

When to Terminate

- Possessing, being under the influence of, or using alcoholic beverages or drugs

- Possessing dangerous weapons

- Immoral or indecent conduct, soliciting persons for immoral purposes, or the aiding or abetting any of the above

- Theft or misappropriation of guest' s, team member' s, or company property, or unauthorized removal of any of the above

- Fighting or provoking a fight with a guest or a team member

- Abusing or destroying company property, the property of guests, or the property of other team members

- Taking or "borrowing" cash

- Falsifying company documents

BEFORE DISCIPLINING

Consider:

- Does the team member's explanation raise any circumstances or compelling sympathies?

- Should there be an action less than discipline? (i.e., coaching)

- Does all management agree with the discipline decision?

- Can you show proof of poor performance?

- Have you done everything possible to help this person?

Do's and Don'ts When Meeting with a Stylist About Warnings:

DO'S: Be specific about expectations

Focus on performance

Make consequences clear

Be fair and even in your discipline process

DON'Ts: Be vague

Focus on personalities

Play favorites

As I have mentioned, you must keep accurate written documentation in your employee records. The following is an example of an Employee Warning Report for you to use and adapt as necessary for your specific needs.

Employee Warning Report (EXAMPLE)

Employee's Name:

Violation Date: Violation Time:

Description of violation:

- **First Verbal Warning**. Date given:

- **First Written Warning**; verbal warning was given (date:) and has not corrected situation. Date of written warning:

- **First Written Warning, verbal warning has not been given.** Situation is serious enough to warrant immediate written warning. Date:

- **Final Written Warning** (give dates of previous warnings)

Date of this warning:

First verbal: First written:

Any additional warnings and dates:

- **Suspension.** Date:

Indicate the behavior contributing to this warning:

- Attendance
- Disobedience
- Tardiness
- Safety
- Work quality
- Gossip

- Unprepared for work
- Appearance (not up to salon standards). Describe:

  _____

- Other (specify):

_____

Consequence Chart

In this section, write examples of consequences for your salon:

> What will constitute a verbal warning
>
> What will constitute a written warning (i.e., 1 prior verbal warning for the same or similar offense)
>
> What will constitute probation or reduction of hours (i.e., 3 verbal warnings & 1 written warning)
>
> What will constitute immediate termination (i.e., 1 warning after probation)

So, along with your written employee handbook and your clearly documented position on discipline, each position in your salon (such as manager, salon coordinator, front desk staff, and stylist) must have its own written job description. Again, this presents to staff members exactly what is expected of them in their specific position. If you don't already have job descriptions written out, here is an example of one for a Salon Manager that you can review.

SALON MANAGER JOB DESCRIPTION

The salon manager(s)' responsibilities include these key tasks:

1. Recruit, hire and schedule salon staff.

- Recruit
- Interview
- Hire
- Set up work schedules

2. Oversee training of salon staff.

- Schedule stylists to class
- Handle new team member orientation
- Consistently coach for better skills

- Train thoroughly in safety issues

3. Evaluate performance of salon staff.

- Evaluate
- Discipline
- Promote
- Terminate

4. Effectively motivate all staff.

- Staff meetings
- Promotions and contests
- Formal and informal recognition

5. Promote excellence in customer service.

- Constant training and emphasis
- Customer relations, tracking, complaints, redo's

6. Control cash functions.

- Daily deposits, inventorying, refunds

7. Manage the image and appearance of the salon.

- Adhere to Quality Assurance standards, both for stylist appearance and salon appearance

8. Build the growth and profit of the salon.

- Promotions
- Attend technical classes (one per month or whenever available in your region)
- Attend manager classes – regional and national

At this point you should have written down how you want things to be done and what you expect of each potential employee before they even start.

THE KEY, before they start. By providing written expectations, you can better gauge applicants by their reaction to these expectations, and you also give applicants a clear understanding of whether your salon is a good fit for them. The more information you can provide up front, the better it will be in the long run.

Let the interview begin. Have all your questions written out before hand and make sure you read the applicant's resume first so you can elaborate and familiarize yourself with their background, skills and experience.

- Open the interview by talking about your salon.

- State exactly what the job is and exactly what you are looking for as far as hours and skills.

- Go over all of the applicant's qualifications, work history, if any, and whether or not this applicant has the basic requirements and type of background for the position you are looking to fill.

- Is the personality of the candidate that of a team player?

- Did he/she come professionally dressed and groomed for the interview?

- Carefully explain what your expectations are for the position, such as dress code, flexible hours, mandatory weekends, etc.

- If you have a set pay scale, share what your compensation package is and discuss their past compensation and what you are offering.

- Explain any retailing expectations you may have for them, including percentages. Be clear about what type of production per hour you are looking for, making sure they fully understand what you are asking of them.

- If you are interested in the candidate, then you can ask for references and permission to check them. Please CALL THEM. It can save you so many headaches in the future.

- Now to close the interview, ask if there are any questions. Tell them whom to call if they have questions. If you know they are a strong candidate, and then set up a technical interview next. If you are unsure at this point, state that you have other candidates to interview, and you will call them back in x number of days, either way.

A technical interview is very important, and it is an element that is so often overlooked. It can save you major headaches down the road. Even if the stylist is seasoned, he or she may be weak in certain areas such as chemical services, men's cuts, perms, etc. I recommend you have the applicant bring in a model, and you should also have a mannequin available for them to place foils, perm rods, rollers, etc. It will give you an idea of what additional training, if any, may be necessary to bring the stylist up to expectations.

Something else I would do was let my manager sit in on the interview so we could compare notes after. I often times included my staff as well in meeting the new candidate and then getting their feedback. This made them feel part of the hiring process, and they were more apt to accept and invite the stylist readily because they felt part of the final decision. A team mentality for everyone is a must in order for a salon to do well.

When you hire a stylist, I strongly recommend you offer at least a week of orientation. Walk them through all you want them to know about the salon and how things function. Designate a senior stylist to take the new stylists under his/her wing to become familiar with where everything is. If the new stylist needs some form of education, this is the time to incorporate it. I always positioned my new stylist's styling station next to a senior stylist or my manager. This buddy system is a great way to make the new stylist comfortable and less nervous. When the new stylist is not servicing a client, he/ she can observe the technical skills of the mentoring stylist.

Preparation is the key to success in getting the right staff in your salon.

Now let's address how to develop staff loyalty and how to help them want to be the very best they can be once you have hired them. I learned early on that appreciation goes a long way.

I used to have my staff decorate a bag of their choice, and I would hang the bags in the back room. About once a week, either I, or my manager, would write a special note to each stylist that was positive and expressing appreciation, and place it in her bag. I would have a pizza party just to say "thank you" once a month. I would get $10 gas cards or coffee shop cards to show appreciation for a particular stylist who was doing a great job. Showing appreciation to your staff can be as simple as a kind word, making them feel special. I treated my staff with respect, and I expected that my staff would be respectful to me, and to each other, in return.

Be sure that when a problem arises to nip it in the bud as soon as possible by having a one-on-one meeting with the particular staff member to stop whatever is happening so it won't spread throughout the salon.

It takes time to get a great staff, so it should be a priority for salon owners and managers to KEEP their great staff. It is our job as a salon owner or manager to understand how each individual differs and to learn how to deal with different types of personalities, all whom carry different issues with them into your salon.

I truly believe we, salon professionals, choose this field in the first place because we have open and willing hearts, and we honestly want to make people feel better about themselves. We feel rewarded from doing for others. However, there are times when we allow ourselves to get caught up in everyday problems, negativities, and old destructive thought patterns. Having different personalities all trying to work in sync under the same roof of a salon takes great skill. If you, the salon owner, understand the importance of recognizing that we all have weaknesses, imperfections, and differences and are willing to be patient and proactive in dealing with problems (and don't ignore them, hoping they will go away), you are way ahead of the game. If you can make it a priority to utilize your position as owner or manager to honestly help each individual in your salon achieve personal and business success, all else will fall into place. The rest is fundamental: One-on-one meetings, setting goals, praise, appreciation, and getting to know each person that is working for you on an individual level.

So remember, when it comes to retaining a loyal staff:

Management fails when they fail to provide...

- clarity about expectations

- clarity about career development and earning potential

- regular feedback about performance

- regular scheduled huddles/meetings

- a framework within which the employee perceives they can succeed

- clear communication about expectations to the employee

- frequent feedback and make the employee feel valued

- sharing of their ideas of what contributes to the success of the employee

Managers retain staff when they...

- praise

- pay employees fairly and well

- treat each and every employee with respect

- show them that you care about their accomplishments and attempts

- clearly communicate goals, responsibilities and expectations

- recognize performance appropriately and consistently

- involve employees in plans and decisions, especially those that affect them

- create opportunities for employees to learn and grow

- actively listen to employees' concerns – both work related and personal

- share information promptly, openly and clearly

- celebrate successes and milestones reached

Why stylists say they stay at a certain salon...

- exciting and challenging work

- career growth

- working with great people

- fair pay

- supportive management

- being recognized/valued

- benefits

- making a difference

- pride in the organization

- great work environment

- autonomy/creativity

- flexibility

- job stability

- fun environment

- loyalty of management to staff

This brings us back to the question I asked earlier: Are you working IN your business or ON your business? You need the time to work ON your business in order to be successful, and much of that time is spent dealing with staff. Being a salon owner involves so many different facets, and I certainly hope you have learned some new things to try. I also hope this book will help you get organized; stay focused, and will guide you as you grow your salon to become the absolute best it can be!

My Action Plan for Creating a Loyal Staff

What first change will you make in your current practice for hiring and retaining staff?

_____

_____

_____

_____

List the steps you will take to implement this change.

_____

_____

_____

_____

List other changes you will make in your staff hiring and retention practices in the order in which you will implement them.

_____

_____

_____

_____

_____

_____

_____

On separate sheets of paper: If you do not already have a salon policy handbook, list the expectations and rules you would like your staff to follow. Next compose a consequence list. Be sure to clearly state your expectations of all behaviors that you consider to be unacceptable and then clearly connect the consequence, or sequence of consequences, that staff can expect if the specific salon policy is not followed. Type your handbook and copy or print it for all staff.

On separate sheets of paper: If you do not already have written job descriptions for each staff position in your salon, put those descriptions in writing. Be sure each staff member receives a copy.

Take your time when writing your policy handbook and job descriptions so that you can include as much information as possible. The more detailed you are, the easier it will be for you and your staff going forward.

We have covered a tremendous amount of information in this chapter, *The ABC's of Operating Your Salon*. We' ve discussed finances, goals and incentives, and we have covered how to develop and write action plans. We' ve looked at time and money wasters, and we' ve discussed the art of advertising. We have gone over suggestions for hiring, and retaining, a loyal staff. Please enjoy my other books, *Top Secret, Retailing in Action, Hush Royalty is Walking Through the Door, and Stylists are Business Owners Too.*

ABOUT THE AUTHOR

Jeanne Degen is a leader in the beauty industry. For 33 years, she has brought her expertise to salons, manufacturers and distributorships as an educator, a trainer, a stylist and as a successful salon owner. Now she has created Positive Salon Strategies, a salon consulting company that delivers easily accessible, proven business strategies to salon professionals in the beauty profession.

Her 10-minute online workshops are designed as easy to follow, step-by- step instructional programs that allow salon professionals to learn effective techniques for business success. The workshops feature tips and strategies that Jeanne herself used to manage and grow her salon business. She knows how hectic running a salon can be, and she is confident and excited that the short format instruction provided by Positive Salon Strategies will help others to be more successful at operating their businesses.

Jeanne brings impressive professional experience to bear in her company. As Director of Operations and Education at Fantastic Sam's International Corp, she has assisted franchisees nationwide to build salon revenue. She not only offered education and operational support to established salons, but also supervised and conducted new salon opening trainings, including interviewing and hiring new staff. She has taught and created workshops that address employee turnover, that motivate staff to sell, create winning salon promotions, power re- tailing, and that help create great customer service, among many other topics. Jeanne also consulted with salon owners and franchisees on profitability, inventory control, client retention, and all business aspects necessary for operating a successful salon.

Jeanne has also held positions at internationally acclaimed companies, including various beauty distributors, National Director of Education at ISO and National Education and Sales Manager at Helene Curtis. She has hands-on stylist experience and has performed platform work with some of the most elite platform artists in the industry. Most importantly, Jeanne is thrilled to realize her dream of supporting the growth and prosperity of the salon community through her company, Positive Salon Strategies.